ANCIENT ICE

What Glaciers Reveal About Climate Change

by Golriz Golkar

Consultant:
Dr. Leigh A. Stearns
Professor
Department of Geology
University of Kansas

CAPSTONE PRESS
a capstone imprint

Published by Capstone Press, an imprint of Capstone
1710 Roe Crest Drive, North Mankato, Minnesota 56003
capstonepub.com

Library of Congress Cataloging-in-Publication Data is available on
the Library of Congress website.

ISBN: 9781669060802 (hardcover)
ISBN: 9781669060758 (paperback)
ISBN: 9781669060765 (ebook PDF)

Summary: Glaciers have been around for a long time. Many formed during the last ice
age, about 20,000 years ago. They have shaped Earth's landscape, help cool the planet, and
provide living things with fresh water—all while weathering changes in Earth's climate.
Studying glaciers can tell us a lot about how Earth's climate has shifted over time, how
human activities are impacting the climate, and what might occur in the future. Packed with
information, vibrant photos, and hands-on activities, this book helps students learn about
glaciers, how they're changing, and what that might mean for the planet's future.

Editorial Credits
Editor: Ericka Smith; Designer: Tracy Davies; Media Researcher: Svetlana Zhurkin;
Production Specialist: Katy LaVigne

Image Credits
Getty Images: Andrew Peacock, 19, EyeEm/Jorge Gobbi, cover (top and bottom), Joe Raedle,
18; International Thwaites Glacier Collaboration: James Kirkham, 22, 23; NASA Earth
Observatory image by Lauren Dauphin using Landsat data from the U.S. Geological Survey:
21; Shutterstock: Artisticco, 10, Daniel Prudek, 24, 25, Earl D. Walker, 27, GoodStudio
(iceberg), back cover and throughout, Guitar photographer, 29, jet 67, 6, K_Boonnitrod, 5,
koya979 (ICE letters), cover, back cover, 1, Mikhail Dudarev, 11, photosoft (ice texture), back
cover and throughout, romvo (cracked ice), cover and back cover, saiko3p, 9, Terry Kelly, 15,
titoOnz, 8, TTstudio, 26, VectorMine, 13; Svetlana Zhurkin: 7, 14; USGS: 28, Adam Clark, 4,
Caitlyn Florentine, 17, Louis Sass, 20, Wieteke Holthuijzen, 16

Printed and bound in China. 5593

TABLE OF CONTENTS

DISAPPEARING GLACIERS

Glacier National Park in Montana was once home to about 150 glaciers. Today, fewer than 30 remain. The ones left are less than half their original size. And scientists think that within 30 years, most of them will be gone.

But glaciers are not melting just in Glacier National Park. They are slowly disappearing all over the world. They're melting in places like Iceland, Pakistan, and Tanzania too.

Why? **Climate change**—long-term changes in weather patterns—is raising Earth's temperature.

Glacier National Park

A glacier on Mount Kilimanjaro in Tanzania

Losing glaciers can have a big impact on life on Earth. Glacial melting causes a rise in sea levels, which increases coastal flooding and **erosion**. Winters are getting shorter in many places, so snow and ice melt earlier in the spring. This can contribute to **droughts** and wildfires, especially in the fall.

But glaciers have been around for thousands of years. So they hold important clues about the effects of climate change. Scientists are studying them to learn about Earth's past climate. They're also learning how human behavior is speeding up climate change.

CHAPTER 1

ALL ABOUT GLACIERS

What Are Glaciers?

These huge, bright white and blue chunks of ice are the result of a long process. Glaciers are large masses of flattened snow and ice. They build up over time. The weight of the packed snow turns the snow into ice.

Glaciers vary in size. Some are just the size of a football field. Others can be 100 miles (161 kilometers) long.

Ice sheets are huge pieces of glacial ice that cover land. They can be miles deep. There are only two main ice sheets left on Earth. One covers about 80 percent of Greenland. The other covers about 98 percent of Antarctica.

 FACT Glacial ice contains air bubbles under pressure. As pressurized air escapes from the ice, it gives glaciers a popping sound. If you put a piece of glacial ice in a glass of water, you would see and hear air bubbles pop out.

A DIY Glacier

Ask an adult to help you with this activity.

Materials

- a large, resealable freezer bag
- ice cubes
- a pitcher of water
- blue food coloring
- a baking sheet
- salt
- 2 small bowls
- a teaspoon

Steps

1. Fill half of the freezer bag with ice cubes.

2. Fill a pitcher with water (enough to fill the freezer bag) and add a few drops of blue food coloring. Mix the water and food coloring together and pour it into the bag over the ice.

3. Seal the freezer bag and keep it in a freezer for 24 hours.

4. Remove the bag from the freezer and place it on a baking sheet. After a few minutes, gently remove the bag from the ice clump (glacier).

5. Try a few experiments with your glacier. Fill one bowl with cold water and the other bowl with warm water. Pour a teaspoon of warm water over the glacier and observe. Pour a teaspoon of cold water over the glacier and observe. Does the glacier melt differently with each water temperature?

6. Sprinkle some salt over the glacier. How does the salt affect the glacier?

7. Put the glacier in full sunlight. You might want to place an old towel underneath the tray in case some of the water overflows as it melts. How long does it take for the glacier to melt completely? Do you think it might melt more slowly in the shade?

Where Are Glaciers Found?

Around 11,700 years ago, the last ice age ended. A large part of the Northern **Hemisphere** was covered in ice. Over time, the ice melted. Most of today's glaciers and ice sheets are left over from this last ice age.

The **polar** regions are home to most of Earth's glaciers. These regions include places like Antarctica, Greenland, Alaska, and the Canadian Arctic.

An illustration of the ice sheet covering most of Greenland

The Perito Moreno Glacier in the Andes in Argentina

Some mountainous areas near the equator also have glaciers. The Andes Mountains are home to large **tropical** glaciers.

In the United States, many glaciers are in Alaska. The western mountain ranges also have glaciers. They include the Sierra Nevada, the Cascades, and the Rocky Mountains.

Why Are Glaciers Important?

Glaciers help sculpt Earth's landscapes. As they move, they transport massive amounts of rock and dirt. This movement shapes mountains, valleys, and lakes.

Glaciers help keep Earth cool too. Their bright white color reflects extra light from the sun back into space.

Glaciers are also important to Earth's water cycle. They make up about two percent of all water on Earth. They melt at a slow pace. They melt into lakes, streams, and oceans. On healthy glaciers, snowfall replaces the melted water. The glaciers build up again.

The Water Cycle

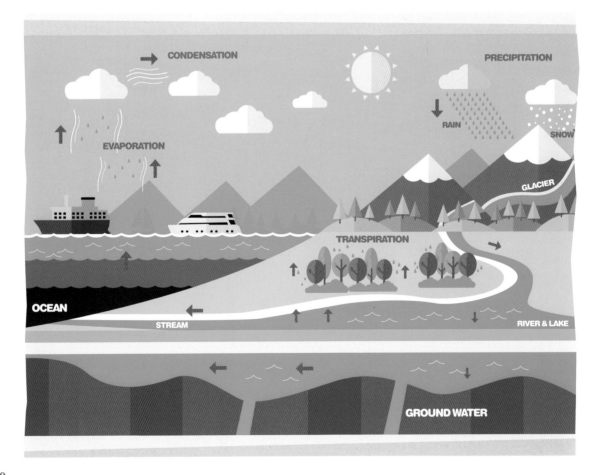

Whale sharks eating plankton on the ocean's surface

Glaciers and ice sheets store about 69 percent of Earth's fresh water. Glaciers that melt and flow into streams provide people with drinking water and water for crops. This is especially helpful during hot summers and droughts.

Freshwater runoff from glaciers also helps keep plants and animals alive. This water delivers nutrients to oceans, rivers, and lakes. The nutrients allow **phytoplankton** to grow. These tiny plants float in the water. They are at the bottom of many aquatic **food chains**. They make it possible for aquatic life to survive.

CHAPTER 2

CLIMATE CHANGE AND GLACIERS

Climate change is making glaciers melt quickly. Sometimes, changes in climate are natural. But the climate change occurring today is happening too fast to be natural. Human activities are causing this rapid change.

Natural Climate Change

Natural climate change has happened on Earth for thousands of years. The energy Earth receives from the sun naturally shifts. These cycles have driven climate on Earth for millions of years. According to these climate cycles, Earth should be in a cooling phase right now.

Volcanic eruptions and periodic weather cycles can affect temperatures and weather patterns around the globe on a shorter timescale.

But these natural occurrences do not have a strong long-term impact on climate. The human-driven climate change we are experiencing now is fast and consistent, and it can be far more destructive than natural climate change.

Climate Change—Cause and Effect

Many of our daily activities contribute to climate change. They add to the release of harmful **greenhouse gases** into the **atmosphere**, which increases the amount of heat trapped in the atmosphere from the greenhouse effect. Carbon dioxide and methane are two key greenhouse gases.

Creating electricity and driving vehicles are two big sources of greenhouse gases. **Manufacturing**, farming, heating, and cooling release greenhouse gases too.

Deforestation also impacts the amount of greenhouse gases in the atmosphere. Trees absorb carbon dioxide from the air. Then they release oxygen. Cutting down trees slows this process. So higher amounts of carbon dioxide stay in the atmosphere.

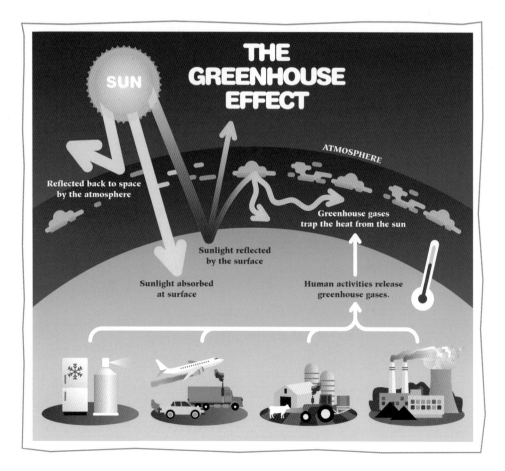

Making Carbon Dioxide

Ask an adult to help you with this activity.

Materials
- 1 ½ cups of white vinegar
- a small, disposable plastic bottle
- a medium-sized balloon
- 1 teaspoon of baking soda

Steps

1. Pour the vinegar into the bottle.

2. Stretch the balloon opening wide and pour the baking soda into the balloon.

3. Gently stretch the balloon opening over the bottle's neck with the part filled with baking soda hanging to the side so that the baking soda does not fall into the bottle before the balloon is secured.

4. Lift the balloon upright and let the baking soda drop into the vinegar in the bottle.

5. Watch the vinegar and baking soda mixture bubble as the balloon inflates with carbon dioxide.

Greenhouse gases in the air trap heat from the sun. Earth becomes warmer. As the planet warms up, weather patterns change. Storms get stronger, and they happen more frequently. Flooding can be a big problem. Destructive hurricanes may occur too. These types of weather events can make it difficult for plants, animals, and people to survive.

Damage in Florida from Hurricane Michael in 2018

Climate Change and Melting Glaciers

As the planet grows hotter, glaciers melt into warmer ocean waters. This adds more fresh water to the oceans. This fresh water makes the ocean water less dense. Ocean currents slow and cool down. This changes weather patterns.

As glaciers melt into the oceans, sea levels rise. This can cause flooding and coastal erosion. Coastal towns may be damaged or destroyed. Plants and farms can be destroyed. And animals may lose their homes and plant food sources.

The black-footed albatross, which builds its nest on beaches, is at risk of losing its habitat from flooding if sea levels rise.

A scientist studying Sperry Glacier in Glacier National Park

When glaciers melt, there is less ice to reflect heat back into the atmosphere. Instead, sunlight warms the land. This makes air temperatures warmer. Animals and plants cannot always adapt. And some areas can become too warm for people to live there.

Changes in glaciers caused by climate change can have a huge impact on life on Earth. By studying glaciers, scientists can learn how Earth's climate is changing. And they can make predictions about climate change's impact in the future.

CHAPTER 3

LEARNING FROM ANCIENT ICE

Glaciologists have plenty to learn about climate change from glaciers. A few recent studies have helped them understand how temperature changes have affected glaciers and how this might impact them—and us—in the future.

Particles in the Ice

Glaciologists often study ice samples to look for natural particles that tell them about climate change. They use instruments that check the ice for traces of salt, dirt, volcanic ash, metals, and other materials. Volcanic ash reveals when an eruption took place, potentially impacting global temperatures. Dust can show where deserts used to be. Salt can indicate that a glacier used to be much closer to salty ocean waters. These particles give clues about what future weather patterns we can expect.

Ice samples also contain oxygen. Measuring different types of oxygen—"light" oxygen and "heavy" oxygen—in a sample can tell glaciologists what the planet's temperature was when the ice formed. This is because warmer temperatures are needed for "heavy" oxygen to evaporate.

Huge chunks of ice breaking off of South Sawyer Glacier in Alaska

Alaska's Melting Glaciers

Some glaciologists use information from NASA satellites to study Alaskan glaciers. They study the glaciers' gravity.

The more mass a glacier has, the more gravity it exerts. Changes to a glacier's gravity means that it has gained or lost mass. Glaciers lose mass by breaking up or melting.

One study found that Alaskan glaciers are losing more mass per year than glaciers in other regions.

Another study analyzed the speed at which Alaskan glaciers are melting. Scientists found that these glaciers are melting quickly on the surface and underwater. Underwater, they are melting 100 times faster than scientists expected.

One study revealed that at the current rate, 26 to 36 percent of some Alaskan glaciers will melt away by the end of the century.

These Alaskan studies show that glaciers are very sensitive to climate change. They also show that warming ocean waters are a key reason these glaciers are melting quickly.

By measuring how fast glaciers melt on the surface and underwater, glaciologists can calculate how quickly sea levels will rise. They can predict the amount of coastal flooding and erosion rising sea levels will cause.

Scientists studying Wolverine Glacier in Alaska

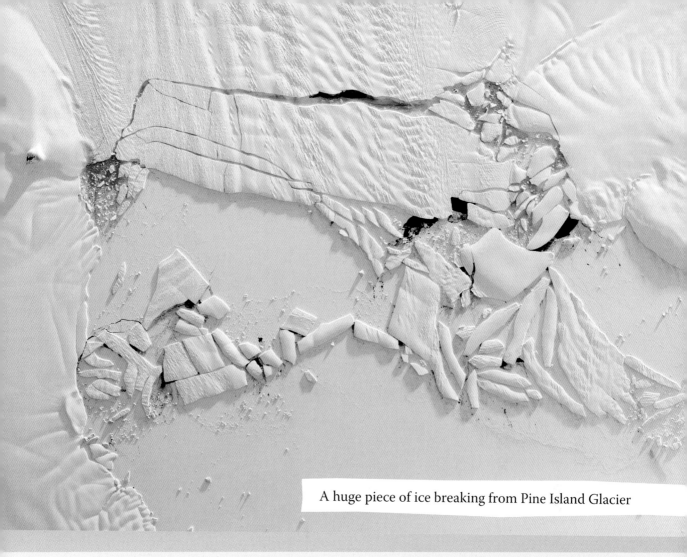

A huge piece of ice breaking from Pine Island Glacier

Glacial Cracking in Antarctica

The Antarctic Ice Sheet is one of only two remaining ice sheets on Earth. But parts of it are starting to break up.

Glaciologists are studying the Thwaites and Pine Island Glaciers. They are part of the Antarctic Ice Sheet. These glaciers are two of the fastest-melting glaciers in Antarctica. Since the 1980s, melting of just the Thwaites Glacier has already led to a four percent rise in global sea levels.

The warm ocean waters below these glaciers are speeding up the rate at which they are melting.

Recent studies have shown just how fast these Antarctic glaciers are melting. Glaciologists studied the islands near them. Determining the age of the beaches helped them calculate how quickly the surrounding ice had melted.

During the last ice age, the islands' shorelines were hidden under ice. At the end of the last ice age, some of the ice melted. It drained away into the ocean. As the water drained, the shorelines beneath the ice emerged.

Glaciologists studied how the glaciers melted and advanced over time and changed the shorelines of the islands. First, they determined the age of the highest—and oldest—beach. They collected shell and penguin bone samples. They figured out the samples' ages. Their calculations suggested the beach formed about 5,500 years ago.

A beach on one of the Lindsey Islands in Pine Island Bay, Antarctica

FACT Scientists can determine the ages of plants and animals using a method called radiocarbon dating. When animals die, they stop absorbing carbon-14 from the environment. The carbon-14 already in their bodies starts to decay at a steady rate. By measuring the amount of undecayed carbon-14 in their bodies, scientists can calculate how long ago animals died.

Scientists studying a beach on one of the Lindsey Islands

Using this information, glaciologists determined that until about 30 years ago, ice melted away slowly. It exposed the shoreline at a rate of about 3 to 4 millimeters per year.

In the past 30 years, however, the shoreline grew about 41 mm each year. This proved that the glaciers melted much faster in the past three decades than they did for thousands of years before. Glaciologists worry that these fast-melting glaciers will continue to raise global sea levels.

An Evaporating Glacier near Mount Everest

Stretching up toward one of the highest places on Earth—Mount Everest in the Himalayas—is the South Col Glacier. Temperatures are so cold there that ice does not melt. But despite its extremely high **altitude**, the South Col Glacier is shrinking.

How is that possible? Scientists found that the air near the top of Mount Everest is getting warmer because of climate change. Warmer air holds more moisture, even if temperatures are below freezing. As winds blow against the icy glacier, the ice turns into **water vapor**. Its moisture is then absorbed by the warmer air.

This process is moving so fast that the South Col Glacier is losing decades of ice buildup every year. At this rate, the South Col Glacier will disappear within 30 years.

The South Col Glacier

Climbers moving across a glacier near Mount Everest

As the South Col Glacier melts, people living near it in the Himalayas will struggle. Glacier melt provides drinking water, particularly during the dry seasons. People will lose access to drinking water. And they won't have the water they need to grow crops.

Mount Everest will become more dangerous to climb too. Melting ice exposes rock and slippery, thin ice. Climbers will have trouble getting to the top.

The South Col Glacier studies proved that even glaciers at high altitudes are sensitive to climate change. They can still melt. That means that climate change is driving glacial melt more than scientists thought.

CHAPTER 4

GLACIERS IN THE FUTURE

The **UNESCO World Heritage sites** include 18,600 glaciers around the world. The list includes glaciers in places like Mount Kilimanjaro, Yosemite, and the Alps. One-third of these glaciers will melt within three decades. This will happen even if people slow down climate change.

The Great Aletsch Glacier in the Alps

Cornfields damaged by drought

But we can still save other glaciers from melting. Scientists say that **global warming** must not pass 1.5 degrees Celsius (2.7 degrees Fahrenheit) by the end of the century. By staying below this temperature, we can reduce global disasters.

But Earth is on track to see a higher increase. The number is more like 2.4 to 2.6°C (4.3 to 4.7°F). If glaciers continue to disappear at this rate, it will cause huge problems. Land will flood. Human and animal homes will be lost. More droughts will occur. And there will be less water and food available.

To stop glaciers from melting so quickly, people need to slow climate change. As we better understand climate change, we can come up with more creative solutions.

That's why studying changes in glaciers and other **phenomena** is so important. The more we know about why glaciers are melting, cracking, and even evaporating in low temperatures, the better we can protect them. The ancient ice in glaciers holds the water we need to sustain life. Preserving these glaciers is important to keeping our planet healthy for the future.

GLOSSARY

altitude (AL-ti-tood)—how high a place is above sea level or Earth's surface

atmosphere (AT-muhss-fihr)—the mixture of gases that surrounds Earth

climate change (KLY-muht CHAYNJ)—a significant change in Earth's climate over a period of time

deforestation (dee-FOR-ist-ay-shuhn)—the removal of trees

drought (DROUT)—a long period of weather with little or no rainfall

erosion (i-ROH-zhuhn)—the wearing away of land by water or wind

food chain (FOOD CHAYN)—a series of organisms in which each one in the series eats the one before it

glaciologist (glay-shee-OL-uh-jist)—a scientist who studies glaciers

global warming (GLOH-buhl WARM-ing)—a rise in the average worldwide temperature

greenhouse gas (GREEN-houss GASS)—a gas in a planet's atmosphere that traps heat energy from the sun

hemisphere (HEM-uhss-feer)—one half of Earth; the equator divides Earth into northern and southern hemispheres

ice sheet (AHYS SHEET)—a large piece of glacial ice that covers land

manufacturing (man-yuh-FAK-chur-ing)—the process of producing goods, often in factories

phenomenon (fe-NOM-uh-non)—something very unusual or remarkable

phytoplankton (fite-oh-PLANGK-tuhn)—different kinds of one-celled organisms that live in water and provide food for larger creatures

polar (POH-lur)—having to do with the icy regions around the North or South Pole

tropical (TRAH-pi-kuhl)—of or near the equator; in weather, hot and humid

UNESCO World Heritage site (you-NES-koh WURLD HER-uh-tij SITE)—a site chosen by an international governing body for its cultural, scientific, or historic importance

water vapor (WAH-tur VAY-pur)—water in gas form; water vapor is one of many invisible gases in the air

READ MORE

Allman, Barbara. *Glaciers*. New York: Enslow Publishing, 2020.

Kissock, Heather. *Glacier*. New York: AV2, 2022.

Parker, Katie. *Glacier National Park*. North Mankato, MN: Capstone, 2019.

INTERNET SITES

NASA: 10 Interesting Things About Glaciers
climatekids.nasa.gov/10-things-glaciers

NASA: Meet the Greenhouse Gases!
climatekids.nasa.gov/greenhouse-cards

National Geographic Kids: 10 Brrr-illiant Glacier Facts!
natgeokids.com/uk/discover/geography/physical-geography/glaciers

INDEX

ABOUT THE AUTHOR

Golriz Golkar is the author of more than 40 nonfiction books for children. Inspired by her work as an elementary schoolteacher, she loves to write the kinds of books that students are excited to read. Golriz holds a B.A. in American literature and culture from UCLA and an Ed.M. in language and literacy from the Harvard Graduate School of Education. She loves to travel and study languages. Golriz lives in France with her husband and young daughter, Ariane. She thinks children are the very best teachers, and she loves learning from her daughter every day.